Stronger
30 Powerful Principles
for Leaders

Stronger
30 Powerful Principles for Leaders

By Deanna Doss Shrodes

Entourage Publishing

2015

Entourage Publishing
Ann Arbor, MI

Stronger,
30 Powerful Principles for Leaders
By Deanna Doss Shrodes

Entourage Publishing, 2015
E-book eISBN: 978-1-942312-04-8
Paperback ISBN: 978-1-942312-03-1

Editor: Laura Dennis

Cover Art by Linda Boulanger (2015)
Tell-Tale Book Cover Designs

For Dustin, a natural leader with a heart to help people. I am so proud of you.

Contents

Stronger
30 Powerful Principles
for Leaders

Preface

Charisma may get you to a leadership position, but character will keep you there. When it comes to leadership, the component I am most passionate about is health. People who hold leadership positions surround us in the world—but they aren't necessarily integral or strong. Frankly, some are a mess behind the scenes and show no signs of getting help. Others leave a trail of more pain than progress in the places where they lead.

God has ordained us for more than just occupying a position.

Beyond a role, there is a call to fulfill and we are able to do it better if we make the decision to do so.

Stronger–30 Powerful Principles for Leaders is designed to provide thirty concise nuggets of truth and can be utilized in a variety of ways. One can read for individual encouragement and focus on one principle each day for thirty days, or further if so desired. Leaders can use chapters in the book as a brief devotional for staff meetings, or provide the book as a resource to their staff members or other leaders they serve with.

There are many creative ways that *Stronger* can help people. My heart is that *Stronger* provides insight to build healthier leaders and teams for the glory of God. God has designed us to be stronger, so that we can enjoy a lifetime of faithful, empowered and legacy-leaving leadership.

#1—The Power of Self-Leadership

Do your best to present yourself to God as one approved, a workman who has no need to be ashamed, rightly handling the word of truth.
~ 2 Timothy 2:15 (RSV)

Years ago I read an article by Pastor Bill Hybels that was the catalyst for big change in my life. The topic was self-leadership and he stated that we needed to spend fifty-percent of our time leading ourselves. At the time I was a wife and mother of three young children, and I co-pastored a church alongside my husband. I was also involved in a myriad of other leadership endeavors on a sectional and district level within our denomination. I was trying to lead my children, a church and others in the world without taking adequate time to lead myself. I probably wasn't spending five-percent of my time leading me.

Psychologist Dr. Pamela Butler says, "There is a person with whom you spend more time than any other. A person who has more influence over you, and more ability to interfere with or to support your growth than anyone else. This ever-present companion is your own self."

Great leadership begins with self-leadership.

How do we lead ourselves well? It's a matter of keeping a pulse on our own spiritual, physical, emotional and financial health.

A counselor once said to me, "Nobody is standing in line to take care of you. You've got to prioritize self-care."

I haven't arrived, but today my self-leadership percentage is much greater than five-percent. It's a process and one we have to be intentional about. How can we lead others well if we can't lead ourselves first?

#2—The Power of Introspection

Behold, You desire truth in the innermost being, And in the hidden part You will make me know wisdom.
~ Psalm 51:6 (NASV)

Healthy leaders take regular and realistic evaluation of their overall health.

Many say to a leader or friend, "I want to know the truth... speak into my life"—but really don't mean it. As soon as someone speaks truth, they become offended and this posture does not foster growth.

8

A realistic evaluation doesn't include your best friend or your strongest supporters repeatedly telling you, "you're amazing" and "you're awesome." You may have many friends who would tell you that all day long. But real growth requires taking an honest look inside. **Significant moves forward entail hearing the hard things.**

Andy Stanley says that a leader who is unwilling to listen will one day be surrounded by people who have nothing valuable to say. I'm grateful for my dearest friend from Bible College, Joanne Greer, who lets me know when I'm off track spiritually or need to extend an apology to someone.

Ministry is such that if you are doing it right, you get hurt. If you haven't cried over it, you're probably not really in the ministry. So here's the thing... we try to protect ourselves from hurt and react by insulating ourselves from feedback in an effort to shield ourselves from unpleasantness or pain. In doing this, we have also cut ourselves off from constructive feedback. We don't let the Joannes of our life speak to us where we really need it most.

People who are older leaders sometimes become less open to introspection or accountability. An attitude of pride can develop from having been in leadership for many years, and they start to believe they are above receiving this type of feedback.

Genuine introspection, constructive feedback and action move us forward, keeping us strong for maximum impact.

#3—The Power of Integrity

The integrity of the upright guides them, but the unfaithful are destroyed by their duplicity.
~ Proverbs 11:3 (NIV)

A businesswoman was preparing for a trip and needed to have some dry cleaning done quickly due to her own procrastination. She remembered the name of a store in town that was called "One-Hour Dry Cleaners." She gathered her bags for the trip and headed over to the store, hoping to finish within the hour and head out to catch her flight.

After filling out the tag for the clothing, she said to the employee, "I need this within the hour."

"I can't get it back to you until Thursday," the employee answered.

"I thought you did dry cleaning in an hour…" the businesswoman said.

"No," she replied, "that's just the name of the store."

The definition of integrity is:

1) The quality of being honest and having strong moral principles; moral uprightness.

2) The state of being whole and undivided.

Some important questions for leaders are:

Am I giving the "whole undivided picture" of who I am in what I speak and how I present myself?

Am I true to what I advertise?

Do my actions line up with my words?

Am I the same person in private as I am in public?

As I speak publicly, does my spouse or do my children think, "If they only knew who he/she really is behind the scenes..."?

If I appear successful but lack integrity am I really a success?

Can those who live with me or work closely with me vouch that I am a person of integrity?

#4—The Power of Example

But set the believers an example in speech, in conduct, in love, in faith and in purity.
~ I Timothy 4:12 (ESV)

Kings used to lead soldiers into battle by going out in front of the army, leading the way. Although times have changed, people still want to be led by example. And, they don't want to do what their leader is unwilling to do.

"Do as I say, not as I do" is a phrase often spoken by parents to emphasize making right decisions based on their instruction, not on imitating their behavior. It doesn't work; kids follow what we do, not what we say. So it is with those of us entrusted with a leadership role.

In developing a winning leadership team, I've discovered it's important for me to step up and act first with any initiative. If I'm asking them to give, I give generously first. If I'm asking them to sacrifice in any way, I sacrifice first.

It's important to live by example at every level of leadership. For over a decade I was a member of the leadership team that I am now privileged to lead. During all of those years, I missed only one team meeting. The reason for the absence was a death in my immediate family. Everyone on the team knows that. So when I say, "It's important for you to be at this meeting," they know I'm not expecting anything of them that I didn't do when I was serving in their position. They also know I lead with the same kind of commitment today.

Live by principles no matter what level you're on. Some leaders say, "Go!" Others say, "Let's go!"

#5—The Power of Care

Carry one another's burdens and in this way you will fulfill the requirements of the law of Christ.
~ Galatians 6:2 (AMP)

At our first team meeting, after I became director of PF Women, there were no departmental funds to invest in our leadership team. So I took twenty-two of my very best books off of my personal shelf—not twenty-two rejects that I planned to take to Goodwill or a yard sale—and brought them to the meeting, offering them as gifts.

The second quarter meeting we still had no money. Again, I pulled things off of my shelves at home to give to the team—things I felt would be a positive deposit into their lives.

I promised my boss, Superintendent Terry Raburn, that I would call all of the lead pastors in our district within my first thirty days in office. This was my own initiative, not something he asked me to do. There are 350 churches in our district, requiring 350 calls. I followed up by calling all the lead pastors' spouses, and then the women's ministry leaders. That amounted to 1,050 calls. Some didn't answer the phone and I left messages; others I followed up with via email or whatever way I could. Although we were deeply in debt at the time, I never asked for money. The purpose of the call was to say, "How can I serve you? How can our department help you? What can I pray for you and your family about right now?"

I'm not a "phone person." There are times I'd like to throw my phone out the window! But it's not about what I like or don't like—it's about what the people we serve, need.

Team members, and those they serve, will follow a caring leader to the ends of the earth.

#6—The Power of Prayer and Fasting

He said to them, this kind can come out by nothing but prayer and fasting.
~ Mark 9:29 (NKJV)

As Christian leaders the power of prayer and fasting should go without saying, but have you considered this in specific regard to the team you lead?

Perhaps there is nothing more that speaks love and care to another than the fact that we speak their name in prayer and fast on their behalf.

At my first meeting as director of PF Women, I asked my team members for a list of their ten greatest personal prayer needs. It would take some of them a while to trust me, while others I had walked with in friendship and ministry for over a decade. I told them to share only what they felt comfortable with at the time, and they could be assured I would hold it in strict confidence.

The Top Ten lists are kept in a three-ring binder and each day I select a different leader to focus on. I pray through their Top Ten list, believing God for their needs. Periodically, I fast for them as well.

Together as a team, we fast and pray. In fact, as I type this, our team is on a thirty-day fast for the upcoming THRIVE Conference. We are believing for miracles!

This only happens as we press in together by fasting and praying.

Prayer and fasting on a personal or a corporate level cannot be left to chance, or delegated completely. While we can, and should, develop leaders over the area of prayer, we who lead teams must set the pace. **There is nothing more powerful that we can do than pray and fast for those we lead.**

#7—The Power of Responsibility

For each will have to bear his own load...
~ Galatians 6:5 (ESV)

A re you willing to bear the load of leadership? There's a crisis of leadership in our world today in which people want to blame, complain and pass the buck, but few want to do the hard things—bearing the load that is required of a leader.

Several times I have come into a new leadership role facing the ramifications of bad decisions made by my predecessors.

I've often quipped, "Hey, I'm a Mom… I'm used to cleaning up messes!" (Ha ha)

I've learned something about cleaning up messes left by other people. The first thing is that blaming causes you to get stuck. You can blame or make progress but you can't do both at the same time. Nobody ever had a breakthrough while blaming!

If you're going to gain ground in a difficult situation, you have to stay focused. It is tempting to get angry and rant on and on about how hard it is to clean up the mess you have inherited. But ranting does nothing to move you forward. It takes a tremendous amount of energy to blame and stay angry. And I've learned it takes all the strength I have to come up with solutions and implement them to solve the problem at hand.

24

Leaders and organizations move forward as they own the problem and take responsibility to solve it. We need to spend more time praying, brainstorming about solutions, and coming up with an implementation plan, rather than sitting around talking about mess.

You've got to take responsibility to gain ground!

#8—The Power of Leadership Value

*Whatever you do, work at it
with all your heart...
~ Colossians 3:23 (NIV)*

You have worth as a human being, as a daughter or son of God. That will never change. Whether you ever do anything or not, you have value because you exist and God loves you.

Your worth as a leader, however, is an entirely separate issue.

My administrative assistant, Erika, has worth as a daughter of God. That value will never change. But her worth at work is a totally different matter. If she offered no solutions and wasn't diligent in her work, she would be of little worth as my administrative assistant. Fortunately, I am blessed that she has an extremely high value as a leader, bringing a plethora of solutions to the table on a daily basis.

It takes little skill to point out problems. A leader at our church approached my husband in the sanctuary and said, "Pastor, I just wanted to let you know, there is a soda can on the ground in the church parking lot." My husband was perplexed about why the man approached him about this and said, "Okaaaaaay... did you pick it up?"

"No," the leader said, "I just wanted to bring it to your attention that there is trash in the parking lot."

People are often good at pointing out problems but refuse to be part of the solution—which is of no benefit to anyone.

Your worth as a leader is in the solution you bring to the table.

Leadership is about solving problems, not pointing them out.

#9—The Power of Being Established

*... let the beauty of the LORD
our God be upon us,
And establish the work of our
hands for us;
Yes, establish the work of our
hands.
~ Psalm 90:17 (NKJV)*

D o you sometimes get an idea, and quickly jump into making it reality only to have it flop? This is frustrating. Let's look at why this might happen.

Psalm 90 is a Psalm of Moses.

Moses was a person with a lot of responsibility. He was leading a million people. He prayed this prayer that God would establish the work of his hands. "Beauty" in this passage is translated to mean "agreeableness" or "favor."

Restructuring this sentence, we can take it as, "let the favor and agreeableness of the Lord our God be upon us and establish the works of our hands for us." **One key to success as a leader is having God's agreement on what we are doing.** Many leaders wonder why an endeavor is challenging or a failure and it may be because they never received God's agreement beforehand.

God enables us to do what He asks us to do. He doesn't give strength for unordained assignments. As leaders we sometimes get into trouble by jumping into projects without understanding God's desire first. We do things and pray for His blessing on it later and wonder why we become exhausted and resentful.

Going further in this Psalm 90 passage, the word "establish" means to set up. So when you have God's favor on something, it's a divine set-up. You don't have to kill yourself to do it. He will do the heavy lifting.

As someone once said, "A day of favor is worth a thousand days of labor!"

#10—The Power of Seeing Challenges as Opportunities

Count it all joy, my brothers, when you meet trials of various kinds...
~ James 1:2 (ESV)

When I was given the invitation to serve as director of PF Women, the department was almost $75,000 in debt. The team's morale was low, and we desperately needed to unify. A three-year plan was suggested by the overseers of our district, to eradicate the debt. However, that plan wasn't needed, for in seven months, our team was stronger than ever, and the debt was fully paid! Not only that—we were also in the black for the current year! In hindsight, we see that the debt was the perfect set up for an incredible victory.

There were many components that went into slaying that debt, but one thing is certain—it was a team effort. Our team has received recognition I never expected. Leaders across the country approach me and tell me they have heard of our victory and ask for advice. It's humbling to see the difference we are making.

Our greatest challenges are disguised as opportunities.

At the end of the nineteenth century, as colonial Africa was opening up as a market, manufacturers of shoes in England sent their sales reps to Africa to see what kind of opportunities were there.

All of them but one came back with the same answer: "Nobody in Africa wears shoes. There is no market for us here." The one sales rep who answered differently was the Bata rep. He said, "Nobody in Africa wears shoes! There's a huge market here!" That is why signs from Bata are all over Africa, even in remote places. Bata is known as "The shoe of Africa."

What challenge do you have that you are not seeing in the right light?

#11—The Power of Processing Feelings and Emotions

Even in laughter the heart may ache, and the end of joy may be grief.
~ Proverbs 14:13 (ESV)

A healthy leader is intentional about properly processing his or her emotions. Many people don't process feelings or emotions correctly, leaving them bottled up inside. When a leader does this, it's particularly dangerous because he or she affects so many more people than the average person.

When we are wounded and haven't addressed the hurt properly, we harm others. Time doesn't heal wounds. Only Jesus plus time heals wounds. Healing only comes as we appropriately deal with the hurt, and that means acknowledging it and bringing it to God.

When I was in counseling, one of the things I learned was, "You've got to feel it to heal it." (Yes, I've been in counseling. More than once. And I'm not ashamed to admit it.)

As leaders we sometimes compartmentalize to get things done. We don't want to stop to mourn or cry. We think we don't have time and besides, it's unpleasant. But those pent-up emotions come out in the sharp way we speak to our spouse, a co-worker, or friend. When we're in physical pain it can affect the way we speak. We may be oblivious to the harsh tone or edge to our voice when we are emotionally hurting and haven't given our feelings and emotions due process.

Healthy leaders don't avoid processing pain or disappointment. They delve in even though the process is often excruciating. Being aware of and processing our feelings doesn't mean we are led by them. (Feelings are terrible leaders!) What it means is that we properly process, so that we can lead from a healthy place.

#12—The Power of Replenishment

And He said to them, "Come away by yourselves to a secluded place and rest a little while."
~ Mark 6:31 (AMP)

When you talk to some leaders all you hear is how overwhelmed they are and how they can't recall the last time they took a break.

Healthy leaders don't wear a lack of rest as a badge of honor. Needing replenishment is not a blessing, nor something to brag about. God's Word commands us to rest.

A leader that boasts of a lack of rest and a refusal to take a break is doing so from a broken place within, more than likely rooted in an unhealthy desire for affirmation.

Others have viewed exhausting themselves as some sort of spiritual achievement.

Failing to take a break is not a spiritual thing. Refusing to ask for help is not noble.

We aren't supposed to be leading alone or to the point of utter exhaustion; real leadership is about teamwork.

The average human is supposed to get approximately eight hours of sleep a night. For leaders to be sharp, we need to get regular physical and emotional rest. Jesus Himself rested and observed the Sabbath, setting an example for us. It is important to set the example for those we lead as well.

Replenishment refocuses us, body, soul and spirit.

Matthew 11:28-30 says, "Come to me, all who are weary and heavy-laden and I will give you rest. Take my yoke upon you and learn from me, for I am gentle and humble in heart, and you will find rest for your souls. For my yoke is easy and my burden is light."

If you feel like you're losing your leadership edge, maybe the answer isn't to work harder or go to a conference. Perhaps God is calling you to take a nap.

#13—The Power of Living by Design

Redeem me from human oppression, that I may obey your precepts.
~ Psalm 119:134 (NIV)

When I began in ministry I had no idea I possessed something dangerous—a brain.

More than one person advised me that as a pastor's wife, I needed to take care to never do anything that would make me appear smarter, more talented or anointed than my husband. Early on in pastoring, a district leader instructed me that "Successful pastors' wives learn to suppress themselves for the good of their husband and the sake of the ministry."

I looked up the word suppressed in the dictionary. I knew what the word meant, but wanted to look at it in a fuller context.

Suppress:

1) To put down by authority or force.

2) To keep from public knowledge.

3) To keep a secret

4) To stop or prohibit the publication of or revelation of.

5) To exclude.

6) To keep from giving voice to.

7) To press down.

8) To restrain from action.

9) To inhibit the growth or development of.

10) To inhibit the expression of.

No thank you!

God didn't save me to suppress me.

God didn't save me to keep me down by force!

God didn't save me to keep me a secret!

God didn't save me to prohibit the publication and declaration of the revelation that He's put in my heart!

God didn't save me to exclude me!

God didn't save me to keep from giving voice to me!

God didn't save me to press me down, to restrain me from action, to inhibit my growth and development, or to inhibit my expression.

God saved me to send me to a world in need.

And He saved you for the same.

My suppression is not required in order for anyone else to succeed. In the Kingdom of God, everyone is designed to flourish. Live by design!

#14—The Power of Holding Loosely

The earth is the Lord's and everything in it, the world and all who live in it.
~ Psalm 24:1 (NIV)

Here's a prophetic word. Imagine me singing it...

"Hold on loosely... and don't let go... if you cling too tightly, you're gonna lose control, lose control... saith the Lord..." (Just kidding on the saith the Lord...and the prophetic word part too...)

Okay, here's a pop quiz for you:

How many times do you say "my"?

MY team.

MY ministry.

MY program.

MY church.

The reality? Everything is God's. We're just stewards.

I often tell our team, "This is not Deanna Shrodes Ministries. This ministry belongs to God. And it's about teamwork."

When we maneuver to possess our position, people or an organization, we make judgment calls that are for our survival, not the organization's success.

Every day when facing situations at work, I ask myself, "What is the best decision for PF Women?"

Sometimes it is not what I would personally choose if it were all about me.

This extends to anything in life...

Before my husband is mine, he's God's.

My children belong to God. I need to release them to Him to do what He wants to do in them. That may not always be something of my own choosing.

Truth be told, I don't like every song we sing in our church, even when I'm leading worship. The more we try to control everything, the more we lose.

Healthy leadership is about serving others; it's not about us.

#15—The Power of Elevating Others

So Christ Himself gave the apostles, the prophets, the evangelists, the pastors and teachers, to equip his people for works of service, so that the body of Christ may be built up...
~ Ephesians 4:11 (NIV)

B eth Revis says, "A leader isn't someone who forces others to make him stronger; a leader is someone willing to give his strength to others so that they may have the strength to stand on their own." Elevating others to reach their full potential is what leadership is about.

Ephesians 4:11 says that we are to equip people to do works of service for the building of the kingdom of God.

Healthy leadership raises others up, with a desire for the one being led to not only succeed but exceed.

A strong leader amplifies the voices of as many people as possible, encouraging them to share with others what God has done in their lives. Some leaders are comfortable with others using a portion of their gifts, but not all. For instance, do we hold tightly to everything but the ministry of helps, reserving all of the speaking opportunities for ourselves? Many leaders will look for opportunities for leaders to be used in setting up tables, serving food, cleaning up or distributing materials. But how many leaders do the work of developing people in sharing their story with others? As we tell what God has done for us, people experience life change through Christ.

Serving in the ministry of helps is a blessing and impacts the Kingdom, but it is equally life changing to be mentored by a leader in the development of all of one's gifts, not just a few.

As leaders we aren't called to do the entire ministry, including the speaking— but to elevate and amplify others as they follow the call of God upon their lives.

#16—The Power of Listening

*Do not merely look out for your
own personal interests, but also
for the interests of others.
~ Philippians 2:4 (AMP)*

Listening to people talk about
themselves is one of the greatest
ways to make a connection.

Ernest Hemingway once said, "When
people talk, listen completely. Most
people never listen."

When I first meet people, whether it be in
a business meeting, over lunch or coffee, I
try to keep the conversation off of myself
and the department I lead. It's not that I

don't have wonderful things to share, but it's simply not the way to a person's heart.

People want to feel heard. Through one of the hundreds of calls I made to lead pastors' wives when I first became director of PF Women, I connected with a new friend. We made plans to have lunch since her workplace is not too far from my office. She had never been involved with anything PF Women does. We were limited to a one-hour lunch because of her work schedule. We never ended up discussing any topic other than some issues she was having with her son. I listened and gave a few comforting words, saying very little but giving the gift of presence.

When I returned to the office, my assistant Erika asked me if I had a good talk with her and if I thought she and her church would begin participating in anything with us. I said, "I really don't know. We only talked about something with her family the entire time."

Not even an hour later, Erika came into my office and said, "Deanna, whatever happened at lunch must have been amazing! That pastor's wife has just registered herself and her leaders for our STRONGER Conference!"

Listening makes a huge impact. Try it.

#17—The Power of Sacrifice

So here's what I want you to do, God helping you: Take your everyday ordinary life—your sleeping, eating, going-to-work and walking-around life—and place it before God as an offering.
~ Romans 12:1 (The Message)

Real leaders don't run away from sacrifice, they run toward it.

When I began as director of PF Women I knew we were going to have to take some radical steps to get on course. One of those steps was doing a "Couch Tour" around the state, making eighteen stops in a short time, from Jacksonville to

Miami and everywhere in between. The purpose would be to share vision and mission, stir up a revival spirit among the women of our district, and raise funds. Most of the people thought we referred to the tour as a "Couch Tour" because I shared vision from the stage, sitting on a couch. That was true, but our team knew the deeper meaning.

I told the team we were going to do a tour with no money. Some leaders say "no money" and they mean "We're only spending $1000." Or they mean little money in comparison to what they spent last time. But when I say no money, I mean literally no money. Nothing was spent on that tour by our department. I didn't turn in mileage, and covered all of the travel expenses myself. And, when going somewhere further than two hours from home, I called a friend in the area to say, "Can I sleep on your couch?" Thus the reason the tour was dubbed, the "Couch Tour."

That tour was a catalyst to turn our department around. It was wildly successful and we're actually still doing a yearly tour, although there has been much tweaking and improvement since the first one. I am able to turn in mileage now, although I still sleep on the occasional couch and don't mind it. (It's great to spend time in leaders' homes and experience life with them.)

We make progress and gain influence through sacrifice.

#18—The Power of Transparency

Don't carry around with you two weights, one heavy and the other light, and don't keep two measures at hand, one large and the other small. Use only one weight, a true and honest weight, and one measure, a true and honest measure, so that you will live a long time on the land that GOD, your God, is giving you. Dishonest weights and measures are an abomination to GOD...

~ Deuteronomy 13:13-16 (MSG)

This passage of scripture refers to the way business was conducted in the Old Testament times. For truth in business dealings, people would carry weights with them and if someone wanted to buy something they would measure it against the stone. However, dishonest traders would carry rocks of differing sizes yet mark them as being the same, depending on who was buying from them. In other words, they did different things depending on who they were with.

This scriptural principle is reinforced in Proverbs 20 where it says that God hates dishonest scales.

Leaders often fall into the trap of using dishonest scales with what they say, depending on who they are with.

A few years ago, a pastor called me to ask my thoughts on a subject. It wasn't an issue of right and wrong, but I knew right away that we would disagree on something he felt very strongly about. I have preached in this pastor's church numerous times. I realized if I was honest, he may never invite me to his church again and, furthermore, he may tell other leaders about our differing views. I took a deep breath, and was transparent anyway. We agreed to disagree, are still good friends and I have been invited back to preach several times since.

What will you do when tempted to use dishonest scales?

#19—The Power of Humility

Since God chose you to be the holy people he loves, you must clothe yourselves with tenderhearted mercy, kindness, humility, gentleness, and patience.
~ Colossians 3:12 (NLT)

A salesman closed countless deals with the following statement: "Let me show you something several of your neighbors said you couldn't afford..."

Pride was the first sin, resulting in the fall of man.

Pride is mentioned ninety-three times in scripture, and never once does scripture say anything good about it.

Pride is the major downfall of man. It leads us into so much pain if left unchecked. It's what leads us to live in secrecy, or refuse to get help when we need it.

Pride wrecks homes, churches, organizations and people.

Pride will lead us to do the stupidest things we've ever done.

God calls us to true humility and this is especially important for leaders.

Humility is not self-hatred, nor is it the inability to receive a compliment. True humility is having a proper view of ourselves.

There are a plethora of reasons that humility is important. Most people are quick to point out that if you aren't humble, you'll fall. That is true as the Bible says pride goes before a fall. Another important reason is that there is a lack of significant growth without humility. A humble leader is a learning leader. If we are full of ourselves, there is no room for us to learn anything else.

Proverbs 27:7 says, "He who is full loathes honey, but to the hungry even what is bitter tastes sweet."

Do you want to be a learning leader who goes to the next level? The hungry soul, the one who is humble and teachable will be filled. And learning is for a lifetime!

#20—The Power of Credit

Now also we beseech you, brethren, get to know those who labor among you [recognize them for what they are, acknowledge and appreciate and respect them all...]
~ I Thessalonians 5:12 (AMP)

Some leaders can't keep team members for very long. One reason is because there is a lack of honor for people's gifting and ideas. Leadership is about stewardship. Usually people refer to tithing or administration in this regard, but what about the proper stewardship of our team members' gifts and ideas? Shouldn't we strive to be good stewards of everything God has given us? Our team members and their contributions are a sacred trust.

What happens when we refuse to give credit or attribute the credit to the wrong person? Team members stop contributing ideas at the table. If they are walking in the proper spirit they will not become contentious or divisive, but they do eventually get quiet. Leaders become afraid to share their ideas when they are not properly stewarded. After watching the same scenario repeat itself, they usually resign.

When I present something to our team and give someone credit, it's a win for the team member who came up with the idea, a win for our team and organization. One of the ways it's a win for me is that I am able to keep leaders like this on my team, and acquire many more of the same caliber.

Many leaders want creative people surrounding them, but aren't willing to give others the kudos.

For far too long in the body of Christ we have preached about how truly Godly people are disinterested in receiving credit, and that all glory should be attributed to God. While we do need to give God the glory, it is not a license to devalue or abuse our team members. **Fully appreciating the gifts of those we are given the privilege of leading is a win for all.**

#21—The Power of Trust

Calling the Twelve to him, he began to send them out two by two...
~ Mark 6:7 (NIV)

Leadership roles carry with them instances of betrayal for most people, but even before a leader gets to their post most already have pain to process. Many leaders whose trust is shattered have trouble trusting anyone again. I understand, for I too have been there with prior-to-leadership wounds to heal, as well as ones that happened at the hands of those I led. Unfortunately, there are times that those who never break our trust pay dearly because others have hurt us. We have a responsibility to pursue healing, for ourselves and for others.

It's impossible to grow or succeed without having trust in others. This doesn't mean trust is to be extended without regard or wisdom. But to be effective, trust must be valued and given. Ronald Reagan once said, "Trust, but verify." Great leaders never accomplish anything completely alone.

Jesus trusted a team and they continued spreading the message long after He ascended into heaven, right up until this very day. Jesus showed us by example the importance of teams and trust. He sent them out "two by two." And He invested His life in twelve leaders and trusted them. Even though He faced betrayal—still He trusted.

We cannot build deep relationships or accomplish great things without trusting others. Something that is built entirely alone has limited reach and success. As we join with others incredible results unfold with lasting value and impact.

Ernest Hemingway said, "The best way to find out if you can trust somebody is to trust them."

The extraordinary does not happen in an atmosphere of distrust! Are you pursuing healing for hurts and extending trust?

#22—The Power of Mentorship

Instruct the wise and they will
be even wiser.
~ Proverbs 9:9 (NLT)

Mentorship is not possible unless and until a person qualifies for such. When people approach me and ask that I mentor them and I mention qualifying, they often give me a puzzled look.

I go on to explain that some people are not ready for a mentor. While they may think they want mentorship, the fact is, they do not have a true desire to learn.

When your mentor walks away from a conversation with you, do they have the feeling that you really wanted their thoughts, wisdom and advice?

I've been mentoring people on varying levels for many years and it's interesting that some people will say, "It's amazing to me the things I've learned from her over these years" while others will say, "I really didn't learn anything from her." The difference isn't really how I led him or her, it's in how willing the person was to receive.

The person being mentored has more effect on how much is received than the mentor. In the parable of the sower, the same sower sowed the same seed on the four different types of ground. In other words, the same teacher, or preacher, with the same techniques presented the same message. The condition of the ground made the difference in results.

The disciples had a teachable spirit when they asked Jesus, "Teach us to pray."

On the day of Pentecost people "gladly received the word and three thousand were added."

Paul called those at Berea noble because they "received the word with all readiness of mind."

Do you see the pattern?

#23—The Power of Kindness

Love is very patient and kind...
~ I Corinthians 13:4 (TLB)

It's been said that it's "nice to be important but it's more important to be nice."

In the first team meeting I led as director of PF Women, I let them know one of my top priorities would be to establish a culture of kindness. This included our internal behavior as a team to our external dealings with those we serve. I relentlessly inspected the atmosphere for kindness. This extended to everything from the way we spoke to each other in meetings to the way we received an offering.

Repeatedly, I urged our team to do all things with kindness and tried to be the best example in leading the way that I could.

The culture of kindness we established has helped us to reach record-breaking goals and dreams.

Anything we accomplish can be done with kindness. If it can't maybe we need to ask ourselves if we should be doing it in the first place.

British Playwright Somerset Maugham shared that his mother was "very small, with large brown eyes and hair of rich reddish gold, exquisite features, and lovely skin." Someone once said to his mother, "You're so beautiful and there are so many people in love with you. Why are you faithful to that ugly little man you've married?" His mother answered: "He never hurts my feelings."

Kindness can lead to falling in love and staying in love.

Kindness can compel people to give to a need presented by the leader of an organization.

Kindness can change the world.

#24—The Power of Preparation

Go to the ant, "O lazy one;
Observe her ways and be wise,
which, having no chief, overseer
or ruler, she prepares her food
in the summer And brings in
her provisions [of food for the
winter] in the harvest."
~ Proverbs 6:6-8 (AMP)

Abraham Lincoln was reported to have said, "If I had sixty minutes to cut down a tree, I would spend forty minutes sharpening the ax and twenty minutes cutting it down."

I spend a lot of time preparing to do things. In fact, I spend more time preparing to do things than I spend actually doing whatever it is I'm preparing for.

I believe this is one of the biggest misconceptions followers have about leaders. They see what happens on the stage and have no idea what preceded the event and believe leaders have it much easier than they really do . As I sit here typing this chapter right now, I have also had a day where my assistant Erika and I are discussing and planning aspects of events and initiatives that are several years down the road.

Preparing is important because it brings peace; a lack of planning leads to chaos. And chaos is NOT fun.

When leaders don't give proper attention to preparation it brings an intense level of stress. **Giving attention to your readiness will truly bring relief in life's situations.** The sage advice that it's better to be over-prepared than under-prepared is so true.

Time management expert Brian Tracy says that his research shows that for every minute you spend in planning you save ten minutes in execution, giving you a 1,000 percent return on energy.

What can you do today that will better prepare you for accomplishing your goals tomorrow?

#25—The Power of Proper Motivation

But the goal of our instruction is love [which springs] from a pure heart and a good conscience and a sincere faith.
~ I Timothy 1:5 (AMP)

Why we do what we do is critical in leadership. I believe there is only one reason we are given a role in leadership and that is to help people.

Why you lead will ultimately determine how well you lead.

We live in the selfie generation where the biggest concern of many people is, "How do I look?" And, when they look good, they want to show the world.

Selfless, legacy-leaving leaders aren't so concerned about how they look. They throw themselves into the fray, getting not only their hands dirty, but their whole selves, if necessary, to get the job done.

Adlai Stevenson once said, "It's hard to lead a cavalry charge if you think you look funny on a horse."

When you are concerned about looking good, or surviving, you can't thrive. And your team won't move forward—at least to the degree that is ultimately possible.

Most people ask the question, "What's in it for me?" Leaders who change history ask how they bring positive change for people or for an organization. Nothing may be in it for them except the satisfaction of knowing they made a difference.

Proper motivation for leadership is selfless service for the good of others. This type of leadership leaves behind a legacy that people will speak of for years to come and quite possibly into eternity.

#26—The Power of Competing Only With You

But let each one test his own work, and then his reason to boast will be in himself alone and not in his neighbor.
~ Galatians 6:4 (ESV)

For many years I was friends with a woman in ministry in another state and emailed, texted, called and met-up when I was in her city or she in mine. We supported one another completely. And then—she moved to my city. I was excited! But suddenly my emails, texts and phone calls were unreturned and meeting up never happened although we lived just minutes away from each other. I pressed the issue and asked the big question: WHY??? I was stunned when she said, "We're in the same city now. It's different. We're competition." I answered that I thought we were on the same team but she didn't see it the same way.

There are three things I've focused on regarding competition.

First, I realize there's no one like me. That isn't a statement of pride. It is true of all of us. One of the best assets you have is that no one is you, nor can anyone accomplish things in the exact same fashion as you can. Even if they copy (which many will do if you are successful) nothing compares to an original.

Second, I concentrate on improving my work, not judging or competing with another's. One thing I often say is, "Every day I wake up in competition with myself. And the competition is fierce!" **The Bible tells us to test our own work, not another person's.** We can get caught up in looking at [and being jealous of] what we perceive as "the competition" that we don't hone our own work.

Third, I support others in their work. Especially when we're talking about Kingdom work—we are on the same team—sometimes we just don't act like it, which is sad.

#27—The Power of Proper Expectation

Am I now trying to win the approval of human beings, or of God? Or am I trying to please people? If I were still trying to please people, I would not be a servant of Christ.
~ Galatians 1:10 (NIV)

Meeting expectations is something every leader has to come to terms with. We need to meet God's expectations set forth in His Word. It's also important to deliver what our boss expects in the workplace, to the best of our ability. Everyone surrounding us has expectations but it will be impossible for us to fill all of them.

If a survey was taken of a congregation asking "What are your expectations of the pastor?" more than likely no two lists would be the same. If a leader tried to meet all of the varied expectations they would eventually burn out or get sick.

People sometimes get upset when their expectations are not met and will let you know it. **When I have met God and my employer's expectations to the best of my ability, and someone else says I have fallen short of his or her expectations, I politely say, "I'm sorry I didn't meet your expectations."**

It's true, I am sorry that I am unable to meet their ideal; however, that doesn't necessarily mean I'm going to change. I make a course correction if I feel God telling me to, or if those in authority ask me to do so.

Joyce Meyer says, "Many people feel so pressured by the expectations of others that it causes them to be frustrated, miserable and confused about what they should do. But there is a way to live a simple, joy-filled peaceful life, and the key is learning how to be led by the Holy Spirit, not the traditions or expectations of man."

#28—The Power of Surrender

David and all Israel were celebrating before God with all their might, singing songs and playing all kinds of musical instruments—lyres, harps, tambourines and trumpets.
~ I Chronicles 13:8 (NLT)

The right thing, done the wrong way, is a mess.

Leaders have many good ideas and God ideas that have imploded because of the way they went about accomplishing them.

In I Chronicles chapters 13-15, we see the details of the moving of the ark. All seemed to be going well and in chapter 13, verse 8, they were "celebrating before God with all their might." What they assumed was success up to a certain point led them to believe that the Lord was with them and that His acceptance was assured. But they soon learned otherwise. They decided to move the ark their way; God was ticked off and things went horribly awry.

We can do things in our own power—even God ideas—and be successful for a while. But God's work done my way, not His, leads me to a goal that's meaningless, and often falls apart. **My work means nothing if I haven't surrendered every bit of it to God.**

88

When I am bent on doing things my way, I get into trouble. When I am intent on not only reaching my goals, but stubbornly demanding it be done in my way or in my timing, I start to get wake-up calls.

There's a better way!

Surrendering absolutely everything is the answer.

There is no failure in the surrendered life.

#29—The Power of Stamina

Blessed is the man who remains steadfast under trial, for when he has stood the test he will receive the crown of life, which God has promised to those who love him.
~ James 1:12 (ESV)

There aren't any hard and fast ways to success—only hard ones.

Being a leader who leaves a legacy requires staying power. When faced with obstacles, I often remind myself that it's hard to beat a person who absolutely refuses to quit. There is nothing that takes the place of stamina in the life of a leader. There will be many occasions when you are tempted to quit.

As leaders we move in the mundane and the miraculous. God is in both. Many people believe that those who accomplish great things do so overnight, but it's usually the opposite. Consider that it is reported that Beethoven rewrote each bar of his music as least a dozen times. For his work, *Last Judgment* which was considered one of the twelve master paintings of the ages, Michelangelo produced more than 2,000 sketches during the eight years it took him to complete it.

Often we stop just short of our breakthrough. Recently a leader shared with me the story of a group of miners who were trapped and digging their way out. Unfortunately by the time they were found, they were dead. However, one of the saddest parts of the story is that when rescuers found them they discovered they were within a few feet to freedom.

So much of being a strong leader is pressing through when everything in you wants to quit. Your feelings will tell you over and over to quit, but remember— feelings are terrible leaders!

#30—The Power of Leadership Health

Unhealthy leaders are threatened by the talent and influence of others.

Healthy leaders celebrate the talent and influence of others.

Unhealthy leaders try to suppress people.

Healthy leaders equip and release people.

Unhealthy leaders need to come up with, implement and take credit for every idea.

Healthy leaders invite others to come up with, implement and get the credit for ideas.

Unhealthy leaders are guided by emotional knee jerk reactions to happenings around them.

Healthy leaders are guided by values and principles.

Unhealthy leaders have people who follow out of fear, guilt and manipulation.

Healthy leaders have people who follow out of love, respect and admiration.

Unhealthy leaders are suspicious and hold people at arm's length.

Healthy leaders delegate, empower and embrace people.

Unhealthy leaders always blame something or someone else for the problems of the team or organization.

Healthy leaders are introspective and unafraid to look at what needs to change in them first.

Unhealthy leaders focus on politics, position, and prestige.

Healthy leaders care less about ministry politics and prestige and are focused on loving God and loving people.

Unhealthy leaders are jealous when others are blessed, especially those they believe are undeserving.

Healthy leaders are the first to step up and bless someone or to celebrate another's blessing.

Unhealthy leaders don't admit their mistakes or apologize.

Healthy leaders readily admit mistakes and are quick to step up and apologize.

Unhealthy leaders justify their family being neglected for the sake of the ministry.

Healthy leaders know their family is their ministry.

Unhealthy leaders say, "What's in it for me?"

Healthy leaders say, "What can I do to make a difference for others?"

Unhealthy leaders only get transparent when there's no risk.

Healthy leaders aren't afraid to say, "I'm not doing okay today. Will you pray for me?"

Are you a healthy or an unhealthy leader?

More from Deanna?

All of Deanna's books are available in paperback or as an ebook, at Amazon.com. For more information, go to deannashrodes.net.

Acknowledgements

Erika Hendricks—the best administrative assistant on the planet! Together we utilize obstacles as stepping stones to get to our next level.

PF Women's Leadership Team—for sharing the best ride ever, with me. What a journey, and we're just getting started!

Gayle Lechner—thank you for accomplishing a "drop everything!" edit on a dime. You are amazing.

Laura Dennis—you make everything in my world better.

Joanne Greer—thanks for praying it through as usual.

98

Entourage Publishing—for believing in me and getting my work out there, with excellence.

My family—Larry, Dustin, Jordan and Savanna—for loving and supporting me through yet another book.

About the Author

Deanna Shrodes is the Women's Ministries director for the Pen-Florida District of the Assemblies of God. She took on the role of director of PF Women at an extremely challenging time in the department's history. Under her leadership, in seven months, the department paid off almost $75,000 of debt as well as achieving a whole new level in reaching and empowering women across the state of Florida. Deanna is most passionate about investing in leaders and leadership health.

Deanna is an ordained Assemblies of God minister, serving for twenty-eight years as a co-pastor alongside her husband, Larry who is lead pastor of Celebration Church Tampa (AG). She is a speaker in demand in the United States and abroad, an accomplished musician, worship leader, songwriter and certified coach. She is an award winning writer and contributing author of six highly acclaimed anthologies and sole author of the books, *JUGGLE: Manage Your Time, Change Your Life, Worthy To Be Found* and *Restored*, all published by Entourage Publishing. She has been featured in many publications worldwide, including *The Huffington Post*.

Deanna and Larry make their home in the Tampa Bay area and have three grown children, all serving God and active in church ministry.